EROU

EROU

Maya Phillips

Four Way Books
Tribeca

Library of Congress Cataloging-in-Publication Data

Names: Phillips, Maya, 1990- author.
Title: Erou / Maya Phillips.
Description: New York, NY : Four Way Books, [2019]
Identifiers: LCCN 2019004731 | ISBN 9781945588389 (pbk. : alk. paper)
Classification: LCC PS3616.H4626 A6 2019 | DDC 811/.6--dc23
LC record available at https://lccn.loc.gov/2019004731

This book is manufactured in the United States of America and printed on acid-free paper.

Four Way Books is a not-for-profit literary press. We are grateful for the assistance
we receive from individual donors, public arts agencies, and private foundations.

Book VIII, L. 408-10 from THE ODYSSEY OF HOMER, TRANSLATED AND WITH
AN INTRODUCTION by RICHMOND LATTIMORE. Copyright (c) 1965, 1967 by
Richmond Lattimore; (c) Renewed 1995 by Alice B. Lattimore. Reprinted by permission of
HarperCollins Publishers.

This publication is made possible with public funds from the
National Endowment for the Arts

and from the New York State Council on the Arts, a state agency,

and from the Jerome Foundation.

We are a proud member of the Community of Literary Magazines and Presses.

Tell me, Muse, of the man of many ways, **who** was driven
far **journeys,** after he had sacked Troy's sacred citadel.
Many were they whose cities he saw, whose minds he learned of,
many **the pains** he suffered **in his spirit** on the wide sea,
struggling for **his** own **life** and the homecoming of his companions.
Even so **he could not save** his companions, **hard though**
he strove to; they were destroyed by their own wild recklessness,
fools, who devoured the oxen of Helios, the Sun God,
and he took away the day of their homecoming. From some point
here, goddess, daughter of Zeus, speak, and **begin our story.**

       Then **all** the others, as many as fled sheer **destruction,**
were **at home now,** having escaped the sea and **the fighting.**
This one alone, longing for **his wife** and his homecoming,
was **detained** by the queenly nymph Kalypso, bright among goddesses,
in her hollowed caverns, desiring that **he** should be **her husband.**
But when **in the circling of the years** that very year came
in which the gods had spun for him his time of homecoming
to Ithaka, not **even then** was he free of his trials
nor among his own people. But all the gods pitied him
except Poseidon; **he remained** relentlessly angry
with godlike Odysseus, until his return to **his own country.**

       But Poseidon was **gone now** to visit **the** far Aithiopians,
Aithiopians, **most distant of men,** who live divided,
some at the setting of Hyperion, some at his rising,

The Odyssey of Homer
Book I, 1-24
trans. Richmond Lattimore

Contents

Augury

they'll arrive   at the house
in the poem where the man,
who is the father, who is
the husband, who is   the body
in the earth—
          but we haven't
gotten there yet;

we are in the car
with his mother and sister,
who are talking— people-talk,
  busy-talk, light nothing-talk
of a weekend afternoon—
on their way to   visit
the son, the brother,   after
two days, no word and
the   fear

that lives   like a soreness
in the back of the throat.   and now
his mother thinks maybe
of silence, of her   son, who
has always been a child of

silence, and now is this all
it will be?   but
not yet, there's just time
now for these still- harmless
thoughts, these nothing-

thoughts   nervous nothing-
thoughts   of the living.

because when the car pulls up
to the house, it is only   a house
and not a foreshadowing or
a place of   ends   or beginnings.
It is just plaster and bricks

and a door where there is no
answer, which sounds like —
[what they already know].
  but they have been wrong
before; they may be wrong
again.   please let them not be
prophets;   let them not be

the ferrymen to their own grief.
  let them be
wrong and human and
unknowing.   and if the side door
is open, let them go in

and greet only   the living.
and if his sister calls and there is
  no answer, perhaps her brother
is simply unhearing,   silent.
perhaps her brother is simply sleeping
  in silence—but

is there only such a silence
   as the grave?
because his mother knows
before she sees it—
the it,   not him,   of the son—
      no longer

                  her

son,   no longer
the breath or voice of her
son.   there he is.   and she
already knows but   still
tests the air with the question,
calls his name   once just
to watch it   fall.

Erou

O Erou the kids on the block croon asking
where you from and Erou's got a story
for every day of the week:

Monday   his father brushed him
                       like a daydream from
                       the corner of his eye

Tuesday   his mother stayed out in the sun
                       singing *Hello, Stranger* till
                       she swelled with his pitch:
                       Hello, Erou, my baby
                       in the major key

Wednesday   he swam up out of the Atlantic,
                       brushed off his gills and walked
                       right up to Coney Island Beach

Thursday   the gods of the clubs on Jamaica,
                       the jerk chicken spots and the late-night
                       pizza joints threw off their clothes one night
                       and danced till he dropped
                       from one of their faces, a boy-
                       shaped droplet of sweat

Friday   his Converse came first, his mother
                       set them in the garden and he grew up out

of them like a weed: Erou
of the laced-up kicks

Saturday   his father sat with a dinner of whiskey
and sunflower seeds, spat one out and
here's Erou, kernelled, uncracked on the kitchen tile

Sunday   Erou came right outta the sky,
didn't you see it? Ten years ago today Erou's Comet
set fire to his mama's roof as he came down

23 Madison Avenue

Today, after the cable is disconnected
and the phone line is cut, after
the electricity bill goes unpaid, this

is what is left behind: rusted
frying pans, ceramic mugs, winter coats,
all 27 years boxed and taped

while the wedding dress hangs
untouched in the closet, the lace stretched
over the front like a web.

Since my mother stopped wearing the ring
we don't speak of him.

We don't speak of the mice
dying in the walls, the everywhere smell
of rat poison and rot.
                    Maybe today no rot—

only rooms of undying. Only rooms
of open windows and light, so that maybe today
this can be the house I grew up in:

the ceilings will patch themselves up,
the windows will unbreak
and open themselves to the yard,

which will tame its wild forest of bushes
and weeds. The fence pulls itself back up
and this house, now another,

on Main across the church,
on Cedar by the pier, blooms
yards of perennials and trimmed grass,

pathways of measured brick, the door—
open and familiar—greeting us
as though we never left anything behind.

I.

Gap-toothed Erou,
Erou of the forked tongue
            speaking outta both sides of his mouth
                    believer of nothing   but his own reflection
Erou born in the county of Kings
raised in the lap of Queens
        sitting on the throne of his mama's front stoop

Isn't this how an Erou begins?

II.

Erou without prophecies

    but not without precedent, no,

    on the day of his birth,

        his mother a cloud, his father a lightning grin, and he a

        (hushed)

            cry before the thunder

    Erou the almost

               the first touches

                          of rain

Underground

When MTA workers speak

      they speak   too loud

my father says

        because of all the noise

    nights when storms break

    onto the city   and the city talks back

       above   ground

       across   turnstiles

       through   sidewalk grates

underground

       they gesture and

              clangaclack

                  and

        thunder and

my father once   clattercrash

      once one of them

      once swallowed   spoke with the mouth of   a storm

but now   no words for the dead

     my father saying   has something else to say

       about all of the   all of this

        but his voice

now   a fast wind

through a shaft

his fists

blind hail

on the tunnel walls

but when the train rolls in

it roars over even this   this breeze bang bellow

like the whole goddamned sky

is tumbling down

III.

Innocent Erou of the wordless bluster, howl

of the strays, bray and bark

and Lazarus-blare to wake the dead,

they said, watching

the open mouth like a hollow a

breach in the earth

Erou Avernus whose name the dead pass through

January 3, 2015

would have been

his birthday, 2

days after New Year's,

the day of the blizzard

named for the Greek hero,

his 12 labors

of redemption,

1 year after

the divorce, 10 years

since the affair, 3

years since we've

spoken, 3 years

since the first poem

and there have been

poems and will be

poems but no

father, today, of the 52

would-be birthday

candles, after 3

trips to the hospital,

5 stitches in the

chest, I heartbeat

gone dumb, I hearse,

3 limos, 52

roses for the grave,

no cake, no

celebration, but candles,

52 candles, these

52 small fires, I

body, I wooden

box: kindling.

At the Doctor's Office

My father will begin again. He has bought
a juicer and a book on integrative health.

Here, with the doctor as witness,
my father swears to his body,
on his body, the all of his life.
This is his new start.

The doctor remains silent—
after all, what can one say to the dead?

    A shot of insulin   ?
    Two pills before bed   ?

Or
    I'm sorry
as though he forgot
to write the prescription, as though
the insurance was declined:
    I'm sorry—

He presses the stethoscope to the stale echo of him.

What can one say?

Ode to My Father's Failed Heart

It's okay. I, too, have failed
at the expected, have sputtered
and choked like a rusty valve
in water, have jumped into the pool
only to sink. Little engine, your flawed
machinery is nothing like love. You limp
at last call to the dance floor,
but feel no shame
in your offbeat two-step,
your eleventh-hour shuffle
in a dead man's shoes.
There's nothing left
but the encore, so go ahead:
relax, unravel
like a loosened knot. Overripe
fruit in his chest, you blush
with uncertainty, bruise yourself
tender; little heart, tiny treasure,
sweeten to the point of spoil.

IV.

Erou   a wandering,

               a bumbling,

               a blundering,

               a babbling

                    child with hands everywhere:

                        throw pillows on the couch,

                        bowl of caramel candies,

                        lit candles,

                        glass picture frames,

Erou of the everything

Erou in the world with his want

Offering

No matter that he shouldn't,
that the doctor has already told him where this has led,
where this is leading (we already know),
still he leans over the stove, one hand bracing
against the counter—he leans like a building
grazed by the wrecking ball.

Still he'll heat the bacon grease
for the gravy, gloss the butter over the top
of the cornbread, grate ribbons of cheddars
and mozzarellas for the mac and cheese. And though
he'll carve the chicken perhaps a bit too carelessly,
as his thumb twitches so close to the knife's
inclination, tender, tenderly, he'll rest
the bird into the oil, so gently that even it wouldn't
complain, could it.

Though beads of grease spring and somersault
over the burners so close to the hand, the arms
scarred brown in sloppy patchwork; though
the swollen legs, the aching back nearly give
as he peeks through the oven door; though
he has made too much, too late, in this kitchen
for himself; though he may falter once, only once, before
he brings the fork to his mouth, still he does, and again,
and again; though the cluttered countertops, the sink full
of dishes, the empty plate, the knife blade, the fork tines, all
messied with intention, seem to say, *Look how you've hungered;*
though he hasn't, though he isn't, he will eat.

Hades, Hosting

Every night a feast.
The spread goes for days,
or years: fresh-baked
breads with pomegranate jam,

pomegranate-braised pheasant
and lamb, pomegranate spiced pears
and honeyed apples.
The dead eat past their fill

and still more, beyond bodies,
beyond hunger, they bloat
with the taste: the last bites

of rose water pudding, last
licks of molasses and meringue.
She watches.
At the far end of the table,

she waits and watches this feast
and its host, his mouth, the roving
tongue behind the teeth; her plate
empty, no drink in her glass,

fork and knife on each side,
folded napkin in her lap, she,
waiting, hungry—hunger,
her last refuge.

In her stomach: furious,
inflamed as a hive,
tiny nestling, little mite,
single blood-red seed.

V.

Erou of the house of spite

Erou of the creases in his father's forehead

    the drink on his father's tongue

        the tongue   stilled whiskey-soured and iced

            Erou fed from his father's silence

            Erou son of the shadow

                beneath his father's lip

VI.

Erou of the school of Can't Tell Me Nothing, already knows
what he needs to know:

Street-smart Erou of the words to the wise—

        got a *hard head but soft behind*

is what his laughing mother calls it,
is what his wife will call it

        years later   when it will sound like a threat

Anniversary Argonautica

He had meant to say *witch*
but lost the *w* somewhere between
Colchis and Corinth. The word chips
the back of his teeth on the way out.
Could he fan it away or
breathe it in like smoke?
She eyes him like a cancer
just starting to spread.
He regards her like the first
dark cloud in the sky. Now,
years later, they know without
saying. They have nothing
to give each other but
this: words that fall just short
of leaving, that thunder
like a crew going down with the ship.

A List of Things That Don't Escape Her

The overtime
The fishing trips
The way he sweats
in his sleep, like a house on fire
The way his tongue trips
over her name
The way the door shuts, a closed
mouth, behind him
The night hours that fill her
like water in a glass
The letters
The tackle box left behind
Her shape, watermarked
on the bed sheets, the couches, the walls
The purr of the car engine
in the middle of the night
The woman
sitting in the passenger seat,
just outside,
just a friend
The way he says *friend*—
a skipped beat, end dangling
from his lip like bait

Daddy says

sometimes people do things   and it means or   doesn't   mean

sometimes people are   sometimes I am   sometimes   daddy does things

                        do what I say not what I do

      I mean to say   I did

                    you know what I mean

it means

sometimes it means nothing it means something   I did   am doing

                   you know what I mean

sometimes people do   and it's just people mean   nothing

I mean I just   did but didn't mean

      and Mommy says   I did I mean   nothing

                  you know

      do you understand

      do you know what   I mean

                        you love your daddy   right ?

Famous Last Words

You'll be sorry

says the father of the groom

a joke

        not a thing to be said

        at a wedding

    not like a broad-mouthed

        con – grat – u – la – tions

           for this the start of all things

she can tell by the smiles

     and the up-tempo music

     and the open bottles of champagne

     and the chandelier and the white tapered candles

     and the hundreds of guests   hundreds

the wedding of the century   they'll say

her mother said *finally*   when she finally   did: a husband

              at last   at 22

what a thing to say

amongst roses

    and crystal glassware

to the girl in the white lace dress

    with the cathedral train

to the daughter-in-law

who dances & eats cake & smiles & poses with her husband

before the sorrys

        when he is sorry for and for and for

she   sorry sight, her mother says:

            48, alone; white dress, dusty glassware in the closet,

                what left but the words

I'm sorry I didn't mean it I'm sorry I meant it I'm sorry I hurt you am hurting you

alone in the house

as the TV plays in the next room

a roar of laughter before the break

Persephone, in Part

Each spring,
she tries to collect herself—
the nape of her neck tacked
to a tree; a copper-colored nipple
in the vale; a bare shoulder
by her chambers, shrugged, turned
toward the fields.

They are one in two
seasons, this man
and she whom he took
as wife. Though she'd be,
could she be, perennial: absolute
and unabbreviated, exhaustive
with the full breadth of her,

still, how her body cleaves
itself so generously
for this rite of union and ritual
of change; with each loss,
so much of her
opening and opening
and opened,
                    to what?

VII.

Erou of the idle hands,
      of the Here Comes Trouble
      smacked across his face
      in an ear-to-ear grin:

            Erou of the snowballs at passing cars on Linden
            St. Erou of the stolen blessed wafers in the church
            Erou of the dirty jokes on the bathroom mirror
            Erou of the double-dog-dared bike trick,
            Erou of cracked wall and collapsed fence
            of shattered plates and cracked windows
            Erou of the destroyed
            devilish Erou
            Erou Vishnu of the West
            Erou Veles of the Earth
            Erou solo Baccanal
                of thrash and break:

boys will be boys, Erou will be Erou, eternally,   he is

VIII.

Quick-footed Erou
of the heel-toe push-off
Nikes laced   too quick

        for the courts
        for the swing
        of the belt   (*hit-miss!*)

Erou of broken curfews
of the nights when the streetlights come on

        Erou not quite,
                never quite   home

        always at the corner
        down the block
        tearing through the hood   like a storm

Erou Aiolos of the quickness

        down the stairs
        out the door

                —a gale, a gust, and   gone

Of Late

Wouldn't his cousin love to nudge
and ask what it cost him—
a speeding ticket, a pair of wrinkled slacks,
a wallet forgotten on the nightstand?
And his mother, she'd love to say *of course*
and his sister's head would shake with tsk-
tsks and his wife, still looking
at him as though she's been waiting
all morning, he up with the sun but still,
somehow, kept her waiting at
the grocery store or
the doctor's office or the bank,
or at home, and he swears he was here
first, right on time, but somehow those late
nights, that graveyard
shift had him dozing and now
wasn't he supposed to meet her?
Wasn't it his turn to let in
the electrician or the plumber,
his turn to pick up their daughter
forgotten at school? He wants to tell them
he's here, has made it, finally,
was the first to arrive, dressed up,
pressed, laid out, still
waiting, patiently, for the rest
of them, even now, even after it's over.

33

Haunt

Because there are so few hobbies left
to the dead, my father gives himself this:
his usual route, the Queens-bound F
to Continental, where he walks with the living
to work. Every day he finds a new occupation—
picks trash off the tracks, changes a dirty lightbulb,
makes rounds on the platforms,
tries to make some small use of his hands,
though no one notices
or acknowledges. Yet still he returns
every day, in his tan shirt and brown slacks
ironed with the impatience
of the perpetually late,
his keys jingling carelessly
in his left front pocket.

Twenty-plus years with the MTA
but some other guy's got the job now,
someone younger, maybe someone
my father knows, standing in the operating booth
at the end of the platform, watching
the miniature trains on the board
carry lights through a digital New York.
And maybe the young man knows nothing
of the dead man, has no words
for a ghost who builds a home
of his absence. And if my father says *haunt*

he doesn't mean the way rooms forget him

once he's gone; he's saying his leather chair
now in his coworker's office, his locker
in the back room newly purged
of its clutter, or his usual table
in the break room where he sits
at 10:30 each night eating
the same steak club and chips, counting
the 10, 20, 30 more years till retirement,
because he's close, he's in the final stretch—any day
now and he'll finally go on that vacation.

IX.

Erou who grows like a premonition
      all 5'10" of him in high-tops now nearly
      the height of his father

Footloose Erou
          two- stepped
                side- stepped up out   of his own paces:
already worn out
his church shoes, his one good pair,

so he wears his father's,
          Sugar Daddy caramel-candy-brown leather
               Cadillac-greased,   Pontiac-shined

Erou of the *every day's church Sunday*
                   when you groomed and grown
Erou of his daddy's suited swagger and stride—
           tripping stub-toed round the block

Erou whose mother smiles and says
not yet
              but he'll grow into them soon

Erou whose father laughs and says
nothing at all

X.

Erou nearly grown

      lapels sharp enough to cut
      through the sky,
      large enough to fly
      him into next week

Erou flying high
on his own reputation

      hair picked high
      to the heavens

            a little pomade little beeswax little warning from dad

Erou who has read all the stories
got his lotion and shades
      ain't afraid of no sun

Losing His Cool

On Thursday nights as the Lower East Side speaks
with all of its mouths at once—the legions
of twenty-somethings marching up and down
East Houston (the girls with cut-off tops and
tiny doll purses and skirts that inch up
their thighs and the boys with necklines that dip
down the chest and too-tight jeans)—
my father feels all his years catch up
to him at once and the good ole days pile up
behind him like a stack of old photographs.
So when a group of them—all
speaking over each other, the girls absently
swaying with the same wave of their hips,
the boys bobbing coolly along the outskirts
with nowhere to be, nothing but time—
practically walk right through him, he wonders
if he can steal back time: comb up the high-top
fade till it tests the door frames, sport
the black Adidas tracksuit and the matching
kicks, tongue-popped and spotless, that kinda fly—
can he steal it all back? Maybe if he
grabs a shot at the crowded bar where
the music numbs his ears into a wordless
hum, if he goes to the indie art film
where everything is a collage of sex
and nothing, if he goes to the club packed
with bodies that throng and pulse until he
swears the beat is coming from inside his
chest (is it?) and the sweat everywhere

like rain but everywhere thirst and unending
hunger; he just wants a bag of Doritos
and a Coke for a dollar, wants to be
nudged by his buddies into a dive bar
buzzed with life and women, just like they did
when he was young and unstoppable,
stupid without consequences, nothing
to his name but a comb, some bus fare, and
a whole lotta back-talk. He just needs one
more chance at this, at 19, in a bar
on a Thursday night, to see the years fanned out
before him like a hand of cards—the royal
flush, the best of all possible futures—
he in each one (still there, still living).
Not for the fashion or the cheap buzz or
even the cool—no, he'd trade his rest
in peace, the forgiveness of the grave, for
this: to be unafraid, to be able to go
into the night and return unscathed.

Ode to My Father's Failed Kidney

It's a question of impurity, like how
a lie will live in the body years
after it's told—

        but the body's its own
remedy; it will always recover.

Though if it's a question of purity, it's also
a question of sanitation, isn't it?

You're a type of spring-cleaning: here
in the body there's always something
ready to bloom.

Did you know if one acts quickly
after a snakebite they can suck the poison out
of the wound?

I lied when I said *always*. I lied when I said
you could suck the poison out. After all,

you would know best: the blood holds on
to every infraction. Even poison, once given, is a gift.

XI.

Brown-eyed Erou who spies:

the inner thighs of the girls on the Q64
who don't yet know how to   press the knees together
under their patterned skirts or check the open   V's
                                        of their button-down shirts

Erou Eros-shot
          by the   *hot-damn*
                    of the *Jet* Beauty of the Week
                    Miss Ross, how you swish and switch
                    Miss Foxy, how you wearing that something
                                                    of a red dress

O Erou who believes in nothing but believes in this

XII.

Erou whose first
isn't his wife and neither
is his second,

whose wife isn't his last,

whose last days will not be
with his wife   or any other

Erou in his all, in his only

The Woman

The woman at the podium,
whose hair is ironed back and down
with the utmost care, who wears a dress,
not black, but something more flattering,
thanks my father for saving her, even now,

even in death, though my father seems not
to notice at all. No one knows the woman
who is now crying and has been speaking
for too long now. What kind of she

speaks in the company of silence, moves like a fire
through darkened rooms? My mother watches
the woman, whose every sentence tolls
his name in this room of family and friends
who keep the question of her safe, tucked

behind their teeth. Everyone's smiling,
though it's far from the occasion. The room puckers
around the curve of her lips
and my mother's is a platinum silence;

she wears it like a ring while the dead man sleeps
undisturbed in his box, not a word, not a
stir as the stones in the graveyard chatter.

XIII.

Erou who woos
the girl at the department store
where he works part-time, the one
who works in the men's section
folding striped solid paisley ties

     Miss Face That Turns a Thousand Heads
     Miss Queen of the $3.80 an Hour After-School Job
     Miss Won't Look at You Twice
     Miss Not Having Any of Your Mess

Hard-Cut Too-Expensive-to-Touch Diamond-Miss
Erou, how'd he give her a diamond, *Miss,*

                           how you doing?

Erou sleek as an Ultra Sheen hair slick
Erou of the slack with a slickness
Silver-tongued Erou
     smile sharp enough to wear even a diamond down   to dust

Dido

She wears his name like a veil.

It's unfashionable, grieving
in the way of young women,
says an acquaintance at lunch.

It's unseemly, says another,
flaunting such everyday loss.

She is, after all, a queen,
and isn't that so much more
than simply a woman?

Perhaps she has forgotten herself,
like an appointment, or a meal
in the oven past dinner.

Somewhere there's smoke.

Somewhere a candle is burning
down through its wick.

She makes an extra cup of tea
every morning, leaves it untouched
in the kitchen.

Everything she makes nowadays
tastes like blood and turpentine.

She thins like a tree in the winter.

Somewhere a woman is dying from this.

Sometimes my father is a roaming hunger

which is to say sometimes he's the locusts
swarming the front door or the stray scratching

at the window at night. He is what looks for its
fill, the empty chamber of evening, my father,

who drinks the grit at the bottom of each glass,
devours every morsel and mite—untidy he is, we

are, in hosting the remnants, feasting the spoiled.
When he is the appetite that outlives him, my father eats

himself out of the grave, dines on the neighborhood,
chews our house down to its bones.

The Woman, Too, Has Something to Say

I bet you call me nothing
but scraps, that your mama
picks me out her teeth,

that you know sometimes
I'm hungry, yes, for days,
that sometimes the children,
yes there are children, many
of them, with small hands
and mouths that roam
through an empty house—

I bet you know the house
is empty, don't you?
That I'm the way
the dark bristled

in their bedroom at night,
the breath on the other end
of the line—

but I bet you've got poems for this.
"The Woman": speak me silent
as if to undo a spell. Clear me out
of your throat like a tickle, a soreness,
a scratch. I bet
you name all your demons;

what do you name his?

XIV.

(Don't mistake: Erou loved

like gales love the sea.

Miss Face Like a Happening

miss who happened to him

like a skip in the chest

Erou loved like a storm

loves its complications

how a hurricane loves to spin

till collapse)

Persephone, Engaged

And so the contract: Agree
to disagree—no matter, now,
            it's in words,
                    in dirt,

                            in the compromise
of the heavens,   in the promise
of the river Styx,   in the palm-

press of her mother's hand
against his
                    as they shake
the field around them

                            withers.

•

Immediately the stares:

       the sick, the wounded,
       the elderly, the never-born, the still-
       born, the heroes, the slaughtered,
       the monsters, the beasts, and
       the children, bodies slackened
       with time and rot—

they all lean in, watching,
as he leads her

           down

               and, daughter of earth
               and sky, what else can she do

but hold her chin up like a torch through
the tunnel, the sun at her back like his
hand guiding her, bracing her, his lips at her
ear saying,

      "It's your breathing,"   and so

she holds her breath

for 1 2 3 4 5 —

until in the darkness she loses count.

•

No one knows what to make of this,
the tissue and garland, tiny treats
and teas,

      and she, like the eye
      of the storm around her, seeing:

          dead
              girls,
          dead
             women

      —aunts, mothers—

      smiling with toothless
mouths, throwing rice, and offering
her tokens—a pile of dirty gold
coins at her feet

    (wealthy queen!)

and they applaud and dance
in the dirt, the thunder like
birds falling
      from the sky.

•

And then someone said, not
her, maybe he, that should
something happen

(though what
something, when this is every
thing, all possible things already
happening, things she cannot
imagine—?)

he would follow
her to the skies, to
the seas, to the ends
of the earth,

yes, but
what now, now that
they're

here?

•

She is to hear their pleas first, the recently dead,
who've come to realize what this means, so,
their queen, she is to be sympathetic, comforting;

> *She has a way with them*, he says,
> *They love their queen*,

but the way they plead, for their lovers, their
children:

Just one more year,
a week,
a day;
they'll make it worth it;

they just have this
one thing to say,
they didn't get to say
before they — — and now
won't she help?

please understand; they remember
all of it, and it hurts
—no one said it would hurt—

can she heal them?

resurrect them?

can she send their family a message?
                              just   this once?

can she give them what they were
expecting?
just a little
peace?

can she take
what's left of them
                    (is this all that's left of them?)?

can she touch them at all?

and she says,   *It'll get better,*
even though it won't, because
better is for the living,
so she says,

                    No, she won't forget you   or
                    It's ok that you left the door unlocked
                    and the dog unfed   or   *Yes, you're still*
                    beautiful, even now,

and then finally,   *I'm sorry—*
she says it like a chant—

                    I'm sorry I'm sorry I'm sorry

56

until for days it's all
she can say

                  I'm sorry I'm sorry

for months

                  I'm sorry

in the mornings
in the evenings
in her bed, before
sleep, whispering   *I'm sorry I'm sorry I'm sorry*

and he says,   *For what?*

but she has nothing to say.

•

He'd have her

   dance among oleander
   and sweetbrier roses,

  she's sure, she knows

he waits for her

   surrender in the halls,
     the chambers,
     the forests,
     in the fields,

where he lays blanched bouquets in her
lap, each flower ailing, bowing, hunched
toward the ground—

    but what evening primrose,
     what night jessamine is she,

         plucked,
         potted,
         primed?

No, she'd sooner be kin

    of fire.

And so she'll let herself burn

                    to steal herself back.

Just watch—watch her scorch
this everything, this all- dead   earth.

•

 Yes, for Eurydice,
but for her too,   this
 song, beyond life and
death, too,   who leans into
 the sound and cries and
loves
                              as the song says to,
suddenly, with softness,
 with life, with his hand
reaching for hers, holding
 hers,

                              and the song's the sound
                              of her mother calling
                              her name in the morning
                              on the first days of spring

                              and the wind tousling
                              leaves just outside
                              the window

                              and every new,
                              untouched thing stretching
                              out, growing into its form

 and she has

never felt so half–
baked and haphazard,

and though the song says,   *Poor soul,*
                                    won't you give yourself
                                    over?

she is not so easily
                    taken,

                though he grips
her hand with the firmness
            of the inevitable, she will not
be easily
                    taken,

            but she'll cry
for the sport of it, poor she,
and they'll let the boy go
with a task simple and
impossible:
                Lead her soul back,
                she will tell him, this

                        hero, this
                        husband, whose
                        head already turns
                                    away.

•

She can appreciate a good knot,

such as when she played
in the forest as a child, and her hair,
like a hunger, grabbed everything
it passed until it was its own
forest of branches, petals,
and leaves, and in the evening,
as her mother picked through
it, every so often, a "good knot,"
sturdy, worthy of an old sailor, his
wizened hands,

                              but now,
each strand tamed, neatly
plaited and pinned up
to her scalp, as is appropriate
for a queen,
                    even a queen of her

                                        sort,

            who has scores of dead
fingers to comb through
her, to deforest,
            bun and braid,
            to up-do,

so everything's in
its place, everything's
perfect, immovable,

                until
the evening, in their chamber,
when it all must come

             down,

and he, himself, parts
            her,

            uncomplicates her,

a good knot in her stomach, good
knot below,   there,   below,

            though
he won't keep it
            good,

for he will resolve
her, all of her,
      there,   below,

for his own, and she
      will lie

              still as moss

on a tree, she will be

        un-

           done.

●

At least perhaps something good
can come of this, her mother says
in the summer, as they gather
the fruit they've picked.

She squeezes a peach,
testing its ripeness.

It's unsavory,
I know, and perhaps not even
possible, given the circumstances,
but, you know, these things
are important.

The basket of cherries
sits between them like an unopened
gift. A cherry blackfly perches on
the cherry closest to her—she
could catch it between her
fingertips if she wanted.

We must remember—we must
always remember—our importance,
her mother says, picking

a cherry nearly blackened
with ripeness, plucking
off the stem, spitting out
the pit.

•

He takes her to the end of every-
thing, to the place where cold stars, still
dying, hang low like ripe fruit from the sky,
where the air stalls, stale, thick as ice, before
their mouths, and even the edges
of her (toes, fingertips, the ends
of her hair) blister and harden and chap.

It is here where he gives it to her, the black
diamond like the heart of it all, black,
unforgivably opaque,
                                    but still, the beauty
of it, how can she admire such a thing, how
can she accept such a gift, here, where she, where
the world, is dying billions of times over—
          what beauty, amongst this, can this be?

And he says *I love you* like a plea, and she
tries the word, *love*, and again, *love*, though it chips
at the touch, though it falls, a rock at their feet.

XV.

Erou of the man's vow,
who vows till death

Erou who has no death
to speak of yet

Erou eternally
who loves   till what?   till when?
(something short of forever)

In Consideration of Love

Even now, on some faraway
island almost too distant
to consider, a woman awake
at her loom as the house settles
in its sleep, her fingers undoing
the threads all night, this night like
any other, that finds her bed
abandoned, untouched save
for a dusting of moonlight—
we might consider it quaint, almost
romantic, were it not for the hands
stiff, rheumatic, ugly with intention,
the fingers working without stop
as though the body has no pain
to suffer like grief, as though
the thought has never, in all these
nights, occurred to her, how she
used to have such beautiful hands.

Circe

I magic myself a man: ta-da! and it's done   the deed the
Dirty the down-there down-home hello hoe is me a bit too
witchy bitchy pussy a cooch like a clamp a clutch to turn
a trick a dick *sick hungry woman* I take and take too much
this miss mistress distrust me disgust me wanting woman
wanton woman I a mouthing a tonguing an in-cheek kinda
sly-slippery-snakebite of a woman bite of a woman who licks—
sick, such a woman (not-wife) wily whet-thirst of a woman
with wit tits cunt   *we don't like that* (a woman) *the way*
she walks the hips the lips surely a trick an abracadabra ta-da
ha! I hunger a husband (right?) I bite the beast and feast I beast-
summoning woman beast-loving woman I make me a man
a meal I snare I snake I hungry and I swallow whole

XVI.

Erou who wants to live

beyond his name: a son,

Erou Jr., who will be

        Erou And Then,

        Erou Additionally,

        Erou Much More Than What Was Before

    how his wife will swell

    with the idea of him

        Erou Take Two

        Erou the B-Side—the flipped-over tape

Erou thinks: he's owed this

but the chorus wants to cry,

the sins of the father—no,

Erou, childless for now,   not yet

Hades, Artificer

When she's gone, he reaps
a fresh harvest: fingernail
trimmings, tufts of hair,
wads of earwax,
calluses scratched off
of nervous hands. Molding
with clay and earth these
human scraps
(for doesn't the body beget
the body?), he crafts
a child, crude
and lifeless in his palms.
When she returns, he lays it
on the ground before her,
just like the others,
the hundreds. She buries
each one, fallow,
wintering, asleep
beneath the fields.

XVII.

Erou whose body is a sweetness   (too much)

Erou of the insulin shot

        of the blocked aisles in the chest

Erou too young for this and yet

Erou the last of his line

Erou whose mother prays
he outlive her
Erou whose mother prays
that he live to be older
than his father

Erou eternally but
not forever

Erou whose life is a string cut
unclean, ends petalled and frayed

Erou who naps in his father's grave

Persephone, Rising

Sometimes, in early spring,
when the frost is still melting off
her body, when she's not yet
brimming with life, able to walk
and run and breathe with the living,
she lies in bed, chilled and perfectly still,
as though he still arches above her,
watching, expectant. Outside, the buds
are emerging. The ground, slick
with the wet beginnings of April.
A mosquito clings to the damp
window frame.

Three weeks of stillness
until she feels the pressure, the first shocks
of pain, a wounding, and the blood
that drips, then clots, reddens
her thighs. She breathes in,
wiggles a toe, a finger, shifts
her hips, then rises
to the day, effortlessly.
How her heart beats
with the same red strum of it—
of she, able in her body,
so like the beginning
of all things, living,
deathless.

Autopsy

Blindly watching it, my father thinks the blade
is a beckoning—a *come hither* to the blood
impuissant—a command to the organs to gather, join
the party of tools in the white room—stainless,
speckless as a dentist's office or a museum—
the opposite of the home or the body—*another* body,
that is, *theoretically*, since his body—he doesn't *think*—is
even a body anymore just a sunken — an interruption — of
space—caught, nicked, just so — just so easily — by the blade
that visits him like a cousin—distant but familiar—who asks
to borrow something he will never bring back.

The Kindly Ones

Dear Ms. Phillips,

We at — are interested in taking care of
your real estate needs [we can take this
from you] and it has come to our attention
that, as administrator of the estate of —

[who? will you know him even now?],
you may now be in ownership [you, kin
of your father, in whose image — ?
you inherit — ?] of the property at —

[will you still call this home?].
We would be happy to work with you.
Whether you are interested in renting
[what does he owe?] or selling

[now we come to receive you,
we, your cousins, your home]
the property, we guarantee [as we are we,
as we are here with/in you] we will protect

[vow caught under his tongue—what now
will he say for himself — ?] of your fiscal
interests—no matter the state
of the property [flooding, rotting, falling,

the house of Atreus, of Cadmus, again]
we have a team of talented professionals
to aid you in this time [how long
has it been since you've lost,

since the house, since the man,
do you remember — what now?
since then? after —].
We will assign a qualified real

estate agent [should he wander, should he rest,
we will find him, again, even now, after —]
to handle the property [— after fury,
what do you do with the remains, after —]

in any way you see fit [we have seen him,
we have seen the body — let us feast]
and serve as a consultant [sister-cousin,
ask us how we know]. From sales

[what you've chosen to mourn]
to mortgage financing [what's fitting to note],
property management [as you create him,
with fury, so you we —] to homeowner's

insurance [villainous he, furious we],
we are here every step [sister, we have been here,
have seen him, have spoken the name
of the dead, have gathered, perched

on the rooftop of this house, nails tap tapped
on window panes – let us in let us in – the man
on the couch breathing, not breathing, he was here]
of your real estate journey.

We have thousands of agents [we are]
in several offices [here] across the U.S.
[we are here], all ready [we are here]
to serve [with/in] you [we can take this]

and your property [we can take this from you].
[Sister, we have come to you for the feast,
for the shelter, your guests, we are, kindly
sister, furious sister, we will call you home].

Thanks again, and we hope you choose – for your real estate needs.

Currency

a body = an insurance check

an insurance check = *I'm kept by my father's ghost*

my father's ghost = what is less than a body

what is less than a body = its inverse in debts

its inverse in debts = credit payments

                        mortgage payments

                        unpaid bills

credit payments = *atone for your father*

mortgage payments = *atone for your father*

unpaid bills = *account for your father*

my father = inconvertible, unaccountable, but

                for the body, his body,

                      in a boat on the river, a   coin

                                    under his tongue

After His Death Will My Father Be Beautiful

or will he fade like a T-shirt in the wash?
Will he fray at the edges like the pages of a book,
or harden and sour like week-old bread?

Will he be an umbrella turned out in the storm
when the storm happens—and it happened
so did he bloat or wilt? Erode or rust?

My father—did he recede like the tide?
Is my father more beautiful as water or as dirt?
Is my father the ugliness of dirt? Or
the elegance of bones? And the body—

is lovely what we call it, the body without
body? Is graceful what we call it,
the everything at rest? And the rest—

if we've no words left
to offer, shall we call it
grand? Shall we say it's beautiful?

My father's mahogany box—was it beautiful?
And the pink and red roses in the grave were they beautiful?
And when the black hearse came was it beautiful?
And when the sky opened with rain, was it bright and quiet and beautiful
or was it just frightening, how it drank everything away?

At the Therapist's Office

He has been feeling less than.
He is not himself. She asks what he means
and he'll tell her anxiety, or sleeplessness. Or

maybe he'll just tell her it's wrong, like
when the lights of an empty house remain
on, always on, and no one will speak of it;

or the silence of a TV the moment after
the movie ends, after the credits and the screen
goes dark but still the machine hums—and this is

when he tells her how he listens to the radio at night,
all night, the static between channels, bits of this
and that, and her smile opens like a brochure and

the room breaks open like a glass vase knocked off
a desk, and my father, the parts of him everywhere
but everywhere wrong, the diagnosis she'd rather not

say—the way he sits still as an unrung bell, while
just outside the door, a coughing patient, the ringing
office phone, her brand-new assistant stumbling,
falling. Something hitting the floor.

And/Or

Even a broken clock...
yes, my father's right about this:

he'd *be dead soon anyway*, a joke but more
like a prediction—my father both

the oracle and the punchline,
the 8 in the morning and

the 8 at night on the kitchen clock,
and though most times it isn't *right*,

maybe it's an act of compassion
the way the scene stills, my father mid-

joke, mid-breath, at the sink or the open
refrigerator door, and it's any Tuesday night

or the last time we talked in the kitchen together
or the night he died, cold french fries on the counter,

can of soda by the sink, lights still on here
in the house we have both lost and

reclaimed, where it is both night
and day and everything else and nothing

in between, where my father is here
and is not, is right and is wrong

all in the same exact sentence.

XVIII.

Erou who builds a home
                    a life

        But what now?

when the pipes burst in winter?
when the window panes crack?

        What now?

when the bed sheets grey with disuse?
when the beds wilt down into their frames?

        What now?

when a war is unspoken?
when a home holds no
promise of more?

        What to make?

of the mornings and evenings

a lifetime of mornings and evenings

the same as before

What may we make of an Erou now?

What will this Erou make of a home?

A Kind of Temperament

We're a stormy kind of people—
my father rained for days after his funeral;

we each of us tempest our old-world rage.
In another age we'd have been gods, but here

we are, in our mortgaged homes, rented apartments,
in our leased cars, in our morning commutes.

Here we are in our everyday
spite and sorrow, in our lifetimes of fury.

All our sturm und drang and nothing
to show for it; we're human even on the worst days—

when it rains it pours and we're caught in it too.

Alecto

because a woman scorned.

because there is precedence for such a thing.

> such a thing being the man.
> and the woman
> to which he was sworn   (scorned)
>   now wed
>   to this matter of things being

>   the woman
>   who is unceasing in her —

here let's call it   kindness

              that which is boundless

              that which is without cure

              that which has sisters
                            and mothers
                            and daughters
                            and cousins

because there is precedence for such a thing.

       let's call it birthright
                     that which is carried

that which is born   like a child

that which is called woman

and yes
        let's call it *woman*.

because hell hath no —

hell hath nothing   in all worlds   like this.

Unconditional

How do I speak of her,
my mother, my partner in crime, against
him, he who left us, then we who left
him, we the living, the survivors
of disaster (our home),
how can I speak such a love?

My mother, of whom I am so close
an image, who says I look like him
when she wants to hurt me—
And she can. I forgive her
unconditionally, her imperfect,
boundless love

that pretends to falter
in the face of a daughter
who wears her father's name, his
stride, his storms of temper;
that threatens to leave behind
all mess and complications

(ourselves being the complications);
that dismisses one half of me
to spite the whole. I forgive a love
like that, that loves unceasingly
but with weariness, with fear,
with one toe straddling the door.

XIX.

Erou of the hours

cast off like ships from the shore

        to what war?   Captain Erou

                         of the close

                              of the last boat in wait

Elysium, grant us amaranthine— O

                Erou Omega   ever after,   after all

In the end:

        What journey is an Erou

        through the days?

In Which My Mother and Father Meet for Brunch After His Death

They're in the cafe in the next town over,
the cute one with the red awning, and she's trying to remember
how she got here, in this cafe she's driven past but never been to,
eating her spinach and goat cheese omelette, him, his french toast and
    home fries,
only he's not eating but saying he's sorry, and she thinks how strange it is
when the words come out of the mouth of the waiter, saying sorry he
    forgot the fruit salad—
it will just be a second; and out of the mouth of the woman joining the
    table to their left,
saying sorry she's late because of traffic, the parkway was a mess; and
    out of the mouths
of the boys in the back booth, their faces sticky with syrup and jam, who
    had been speeding
like trains around the tables before their mother told them to stop, to say,
    I'm sorry—
and now my mother's done with her meal and he's saying he's sorry like a
    beggar
asking for food, only there is no one else here, just the two of them
and their silverware and plates and packets of salt and sugar and honey
at the only table there is, and maybe this isn't a cafe or anyplace even
    real—
because when he says he's sorry again, the last time, she wonders
how he speaks with his mouth sealed shut.

Say

Today he says he's

> (going to the store
> for some snacks / going
> fishing / going to his
> mother's / going to his
> friend's / going round
> the block / going   )

and

> (my mother / I)

> > say(s)

> > > (more? / again? / for how
> > > long? / for how long? / for
> > > how long? / for what? / where
> > > ? / where are you going /
> > > now? again?)

and when

> (the stove is left
> on / the windows are left
> broken / the door is left un-
> locked / the car is totaled /
> the fence falls in the
> storm / the electricity goes
> out / the heat goes out / he
> goes out),

> > my mother says

> > > (again? / for how long?)

and he says

(only for a second
/ I will fix it / I was coming
right back / an accident / I will
fix it / I will fix it / I will fix it /
I will fix it)

                    and

(everything is fixed /
everything is broken /
everything is the same
as before)

and we say
                    (everything / nothing
                    at all)

and we are
                    (resolved / unanswerable
                    to each other)

and we are
                    (distant /
                              furious /
                                        anxious /
                                                  afraid)

and we are
                    (family / strangers):

me, my mother and
       (   )

(   ) who
               (undoes / is undone)
(   ) who is
               (at the store / fishing /
               at his mother's / at
               a friend's / around
               the block /   )

and in the end   after (him /
                  the house /
                  all of us)

I cannot say

               (I wore an old dress to the funeral /
               I almost didn't take the day off work /
               I didn't cry until I said the words
               out loud / I signed the papers / I deposited
               the checks / I worried about my shoes
               getting wet in the rain / I laughed
               at the reception / I slept soundly
               that night after it was all over)

I'm saying

        (   ):

            Here we are, though it's over

and I tell him

        (   )

and I tell him

        (   )

    or don't say

        but climb out of the question:

           (Have you been well? / How's the weather

           where you're staying? / Where'd

           you go? / How'd you get there? /

           When will you be back?)

Revision

after Matthew Dickman

There is no woman, no face to launch a thousand ships,
so there are no ships in this version, no boys
dressed as soldiers in armor too large, no bronze
shields forged by the fire of Hephaestus,
no spears or swords sharpened on a whetstone
of bone, no ocean of a vengeful god to cross,
no monsters, no beasts, only

men—a few fishermen on the wharf
drinking in ancient lawn chairs, no worries
but the money, mackerel, and mullet, women,
weather, and windsails: business as usual. No gods
in this version but the ones in their favor,
the Delphic lottery forever a chorus of yes.
And as for the kingdom, no matter, and

no country beyond the sea, no land but this one,
in this version where the homes sit content
on well-kept lawns, where the horses know no sharpness
or scatterings of war. In this version the heroes return
home at the end of the day and the beds sigh
with their weight and war is a word unknown,
unspoken, atticked in the mind.

In this version, then, consider the horse: not wooden

but made of hair and flesh and muscle, racing

like sunlight through a country all his own

and in his mouth not an army of men

but a town, no, a city, of wood and stone and thatch,

where the fires stay lit through the night

but where nothing ever burns.

Telemachus

Fathered by rumor, raised
by ghost, you've learned

to love the slimness
of the shadow from which you grew,

the glory of the myth you inherit—
you can build a father out of this,

one side of a story you tell,
the hero's blood that claims you

in the telling—your history half-
hearsay, half-spun out of air, for

it has already been said:
You are the seed of *outis*,

a nothing, a false wind, trick

of light. So what now
will you call this man?

Poem Ending with a Scene of a Woman Alone

How can she place him, the absence
of his body (un)framed in the doorway of her apartment,
(un)sunken into the side of her bed where she doesn't sleep?

The air gathers, puckers around him, or the almost-
him she imagines, the current warm, then cool, then warm
again like the breeze of a turning fan in the summer.

Even now, in his hollowness, in his somewhat-not-quite, still
he fills the room like water in a pitcher. Inside her apartment,
he's messy, unsure of himself—whatever self

there is of him—spilling everywhere, trying the freshly vacuumed rug,
the mopped hardwood floors, the lavender-scented candle
in its glass votive holder.

She worries about the neighbors: what they've made
of their long fights and loud conversations, if they know
what has been changed, what she considers unspeakable—

What will they think, when she steps out
into the everything beyond her door, that hers is a shape
unaccompanied, but for something resembling grief—
what will they make of her?

May she open her windows, her screen door, to the sun

(though when it catches him, he'll fleck and flicker

like an aluminum screen, be there then not at all),

when every other second widows her again?

Yes, so she'll let them all see, she, mere she,

in her onliness, standing at the door, the wind ambling in:

formless, uninvited, breaking where she stands.

Argo

Enter Jason, forty years later, in the hull of a time-worn ship

(Enter Medea, silent, unseen, in the background)

Doesn't a man deserve a legacy?
A memory, a wife, to carry him
through the years, to bear the name of he,
though forged of bronze, this man, who would have been
gilded, dressed, in gold—doesn't he deserve
to want?

> Chorus: If gold waits in your bed, why not take it as lover?
> (Poor Midas!) why not forge you a feast if gold whets your
>   hunger?

> Even now, when nothing remains
but dark and rot, still, surely he deserves
more than his body, a boat, worn, stilled, staid

> Chorus: If gold grant you youth, steal away your years old.
> If you tire of man's trappings, why not fleece you in gold?

in port, this, his last, his only home, but
at least a legacy, here, at sea, right (?),

he must be remembered—somehow—but does he not
also have sons, a daughter? What has he built

      Chorus: What promises, what vows are engraved in gold?
      In myth, whose triumphs, whose stories are told?

but empires in his image, to be razed,
to fall, heavily as a mast, a stern, sturdy, stalwart, though aged,

                  if nothing left but this,
                  its weight be praised.

      (Medea exits, light as wind through a sail, on a
      chariot of the sun)

Ending

The hero dies in the war.
The hero dies at sea.
The hero dies in a country not his own.
The hero dies on the island of beasts.
The hero dies in the jaws of the beast.
The hero dies with his sword in the beast.

The hero dies in the palace.
The hero dies in his bed of gold.
The hero dies in his bed gone cold.

The hero dies in the hospital.
The hero dies in the shack.
The hero dies in the bad part of town.

The hero dies in love.
The hero dies in glory.
The hero dies in vain.
The hero dies in his body.
The hero dies in his name.

(The hero dies in his dreams but
doesn't speak of them.)

The hero dies in the version
of the story that's everyone's favorite.

The hero dies in front of the crowd.
The hero dies in front of no one.

The hero dies in an accident.
The hero dies according to fate.
The hero dies according to his body.

The hero dies to become a god.
The hero dies to become a hero.

The hero dies because of his tragic flaw.
The hero dies because it is tragic.
The hero dies because he is flawed.

The hero dies because there is nothing else
left to do.
The hero dies because someone must die
and so why not the hero.

The hero dies because it is nobler to do so.
The hero dies because it is safer to do so.

The hero dies so we understand he is the hero.
The hero dies so he understands he is the hero.

The hero dies like the heroes before him.
The hero dies like the heroes to come.

The hero dies and everything changes.
The hero dies and we continue as before,
as always, with our most ordinary lives.

Nepenthe

Let us agree, then, to no longer beat our chests
and tear our hair. There's no need
to balance the accounts or get things in order;

we have been disorderly before so let us return
to the rooms as we left them where no time has passed
at all—we have no use for it here, though we may

watch it from a distance; we all need some sport—
and music! finally something we can dance to,
improper though it is, that we still have bodies

that can dance, and clothes, immodest
and in every possible color, and it will be
the shapes of our mouths that give us away,

the way they arch in the corners
despite—   and our volume, unsuited
to whispers in respect of—

                              how long has it been,
exactly? Is it time yet for the streamers
and champagne? Happy new year to all

of our losses. What a shame such time,
in the end, should go to waste. Suddenly
it's too late and the guests are leaving.

The management, annoyed, is dimming the lights.
We know better than to idle in the silence
but surely we can't help it when

we hang up the armor, when the ship's sails
are black . . .   Now that the band has left
and the radio's broken, let's toast

to the bottom of the punchbowl, one more
round till we take it to the street: Let's all
of us agree to our bodies unstoppable.
There's no music but god knows we need to dance.

XX.

Before the war:

before all is ransacked and burned,

before the wounds,

before the house falls to mold, water, and dust,

is there a hero—a sailor,

      a soldier,

      a king of kings,

      of queens,

      of his mama's front stoop,

is there someone to be redeemed, remembered
in the daughter's song,

before the daughter,

somewhere, even now, is there   Erou,

somewhere eternal,

Erou who spits on the darkness

Erou more than the grave

Erou, my father, won't you speak
        through this silence,

O Erou

I beat the life in my chest
        like a drum,

Erou,

I'm forever calling your name

'Farewell, father and stranger, and if any word was let slip

that was improper, may the stormwinds catch it away and carry it

off, and the gods grant you safe homecoming to your own country...'

The Odyssey of Homer
Book VIII, 407-411
trans. Richmond Lattimore

A Note on the Title

Erou (pronounced *eh-rew* in this collection) is a tradition, a stock character from a classical story, a fabrication based on a true story, but, most importantly, a name. The word is linked to the Latin *heros*, derived from the Greek *hêrôs*, similar to the French *héros* and the Italian *eroe*. The word also appears in Romanian (though pronounced eh-row). All of these variants translate to the word "hero."

Acknowledgements

Thank you to the following journals where these poems first appeared:

American Literary Review, Anomaly, At Length, BOAAT, The Boiler Journal, The Gettysburg Review, Ghost Proposal, Hayden's Ferry Review, the New York Times Magazine, The Rumpus, Vinyl, West Branch, and *wildness.*

Thank you to the Four Way Books team for all of their work and for accepting this epic (beast) of a manuscript; to A. Van Jordan, for all his guidance in the early stages of this book, and for helping me establish a solid foundation on which to build; to Connie Voisine, for all of her care and inspiration in helping me see all the directions this book could go; to Gabrielle Calvocoressi, for all of her infinite wisdom and encouragement in advising me with this project as it was prepared as my graduate thesis and beyond; to Warren Wilson's MFA Program for Writers; to my bosses and coworkers at the Academy of American Poets, where I was employed during my time working on this project, for all of their support and reassurances; and to my brilliant, generous, and critical readers (who I'm also honored to call my brilliant, generous, and critical friends): Emily Carroll, Emma Hine, and Sophia Holtz.

And thank you to a person I can never thank enough, for his eternal love and patience and support and unflagging belief in me, everything I am, everything I do, and everything I aspire toward: John, thank you.

And finally, thank you to my family, for dealing with a writer for all these years (!) and for always celebrating my accomplishments big and small. Thank you to my mother, for her fortitude and love and faith, for everything she's ever given me, for everything she's ever taught me, and for being my real-life hero, one of the strongest people I know.

And thank you to my father. *Erou,* this is for you.

Maya Phillips was born and raised in New York. Maya received her MFA in poetry from Warren Wilson's MFA Program for Writers and her BFA from Emerson College. Her poetry has appeared in *At Length, BOAAT, The Gettysburg Review, Ghost Proposal, Hayden's Ferry Review, Vinyl*, and more, and her arts & entertainment journalism has appeared in *The New York Times, Vulture, Slate, Mashable, American Theatre*, and more. Maya currently works at *The New Yorker* and as a freelance writer. She lives in Brooklyn.

Publication of this book was made possible by grants and donations. We are also grateful to those individuals who participated in our 2018 Build a Book Program. They are:

Anonymous (11), Vincent Bell, Jan Bender-Zanoni, Laurel Blossom, Adam Bohanon, Lee Briccetti, Jane Martha Brox, Carla & Steven Carlson, Andrea Cohen, Janet S. Crossen, Marjorie Deninger, Patrick Donnelly, Charles Douthat, Blas Falconer, Monica Ferrell, Joan Fishbein, Jennifer Franklin, Sarah Freligh, Helen Fremont & Donna Thagard, Robert Fuentes & Martha Webster, Ryan George, Panio Gianopoulos, Lauri Grossman, Julia Guez, Naomi Guttman & Jonathan Mead, Steven Haas, Bill & Cam Hardy, Lori Hauser, Ricardo Hernandez, Bill Holgate, Deming Holleran, Piotr Holysz, Nathaniel Hutner, Rebecca Kaiser Gibson, Voki Kalfayan, David Lee, Sandra Levine, Howard Levy, Owen Lewis, Jennifer Litt, Sara London & Dean Albarelli, David Long, Ralph & Mary Ann Lowen, Jacquelyn Malone, Fred Marchant, Louise Mathias, Catherine McArthur, Nathan McClain, Richard McCormick, Kamilah Aisha Moon, Beth Morris, Rebecca & Daniel Okrent, Jill Pearlman, Marcia & Chris Pelletiere, Maya Pindyck, Megan Pinto, Eileen Pollack, Barbara Preminger, Kevin Prufer, Martha Rhodes, Paula Rhodes, Linda Safyan, Peter & Jill Schireson, Jason Schneiderman, Roni & Richard Schotter, Jane Scovel, Andrew Seligsohn & Martina Anderson, Soraya Shalforoosh, Julie A. Sheehan, James Snyder & Krista Fragos, Alice St. Claire-Long, Megan Staffel, Dorothy Tapper Goldman, Marjorie & Lew Tesser, Boris Thomas, Connie Voisine, Calvin Wei, Bill Wenthe, Allison Benis White, Michelle Whittaker, Rachel Wolff, and Anton Yakovlev.